Sr STANISLAUS KENNEDY

A Bundle of Blessings

ST PAULS

Illustrations: Editione Grafiche © Milan, Italy

ST PAULS Publishing
Morpeth Terrace, London SW1P 1EP, UK

ISBN 085439 540 7

Set by TuKan, High Wycombe
Produced in the EC
Printed by AGAM, Cuneo, Italy

St Pauls is an activity of the priests and brothers
of the Society of St Paul who proclaim the Gospel
through the media of social communication

Contents

Introduction

This book is about spirituality, which is really about being in relationship with God. The dualism of the past saw God as a being apart, confined to the realm of the sacred. That concept of God was a denial of the presence of God in all things, at all times. A truly incarnational understanding of God, however, sees the human and the divine as deeply interconnected. God is not somebody out there to be 'meditated on' or 'prayed to', and our search for ourselves is also our search for God, and our search for God is deeply rooted in ourselves and our experiences.

Practising our spirituality means walking with God, and walking with God means walking with our true selves and being in step with ourselves as the mystery of life unfolds to us. Walking with God means uncovering the real and vital inter-connectedness of all creation and entering into that mystery. If we are in relationship with God, if we are walking with God, then we have moments of awareness of the presence of God and our ordinary humdrum days are full of grace, full of the blessings of graciousness, hope, celebration, solidarity, compassion and gratitude.

It is important to let God lead us to these experiences, to shower these blessings on us; it is important to strike the rock so that the blessings of God can flow out on us. Life is a movement between what is and what is not yet, from brokenness to new life, from struggle to blessings. Often it is our wounds that bring us blessings: our wounds are an opening into the way of healing and of wholeness and we move, through our woundedness, from our closed hearts and self-sufficiency into the promised land of blessings. We go to the edge of our lives only to be blessed and made whole.

Life is a bundle of blessings: all we have to do is open it up and the blessings will come pouring out. The following pages are an invitation to you to engage with me in that experience of opening up the bundle of blessings and opening ourselves up to receive them.

How to use this book

I hope that each chapter of this book will in its own way bring people to an understanding of the blessings of God and into a closer relationship with God. At the end of each chapter I have included some guidance to help you to name and to claim, to call and to recall your own experiences of God.

Time and place

To deepen your relationship with God, you need to give time to it each day. I suggest that you start by carving ten minutes out of each day, preferably in the morning, and then working up to twenty or thirty minutes if you can. This may mean sacrificing something else – some extra time asleep, in conversation, listening to the radio. You also need to find a quiet space to do this. This may be difficult for you but I believe it is essential for all of us because of the hectic pace of life and the noise that invades our lives today. It doesn't matter where the space is, as long as it is a quiet place for you.

Breathing

I suggest that you start each quiet time by placing yourself in the presence of God, the God of your heart. If you find it difficult to quieten down, to be present to God, I suggest you use your breath to slow your mind and body down, concentrating on breathing easily and regularly and attentively. I find that using a mantra helps. Repeating a particular word or a phrase as you breathe in and breathe out can help you to move into that quiet space within you where you will meet your God in a very special way.

Reading

When you are at peace in your quiet space, and if you would like to use this book as part of your quiet time with God, I suggest that you begin by reading part of the text, whatever part of it appeals to you. It may only be a few lines, whatever you feel drawn to. It may help also to read a verse or two of scripture, to hear what God is saying to you.

Imaging

I suggest that you let the words and phrases you read stay with you and allow an image to emerge from them. Images help us to move from the concrete to the less concrete, to link the concrete and the intangible, to connect our inner and outer worlds. Images can help us to let our minds sink into our hearts, and it is in our hearts that we meet

God – not in our heads. Images help us to stay focused and centred. In *Core Images of the Self* Jean Daldy Cleft describes an image as something concrete, having specific meanings. It helps us to connect at some level with ourselves. Each person, she contends, has core images that are central to their lives and are sources of positive energy and growth.

Some people who are not accustomed to the use of images may feel that they cannot do it, that they don't have an imagination, that they do not think in imagery, but in fact we all image all the time, even though we may not always be aware of it. It is only when we stop and let the image surface that we realise how much imagery is part of how we think and experience. If you say things like 'My life is a mess' or 'My world is upside down', then you are using images to describe your situation. Images or symbols provide a vehicle for entering into another level of experience, for discovering our inner life.

To help you to use images as part of your prayer session, your quiet time with God, I have provided a number of questions at the end of each chapter. They are meant to prompt you towards the images that help you to reflect on the blessings covered in the chapter. Don't try to think about all the questions at once. Just choose one that appeals to you. Let whatever image comes to you surface. Stay with it, listen to it. The image may be a sound, a word, a phrase, a picture, something taken from nature, something you have experienced in the past. It may draw on one of your senses or all of them. The important thing is that the image is yours. It is God at work in you, deepening your spirituality.

Reflection

Towards the end of your quiet time for prayer, I suggest that you spend some time in reflection, reflecting on what is happening in your relationship with God and listening to the desires and stirrings of your heart.

Journal

Finally, I suggest that you keep a journal where you write down your reflections, and questions are also provided at the end of each chapter as a starting point for your daily journal. Your journal can be a means of integrating your life and your prayer and a means of keeping a record of the images and issues and desires that arise for you in your prayer time. If you keep a journal, you'll find it useful also for looking back on at the end of each day, week, month or year, and it should help you to discover what God is drawing you to.

Chapter 1

14

Graciousness

Grace is rooted in love

Grace is defined by the dictionary as attractiveness, ease and refinement of movement and manners, unconstrained good will, divine regeneration and inspired influence. For me, grace is the dynamic flowering of God's love. When theologians describe grace in all its forms, they speak of a love so abundant, so selfless, so endlessly overflowing that it surpasses description.

Jesus spoke of God as being our intimate, loving parent. A mother loves her baby just because it is her baby. The infant does not need to earn its mother's love. God's love for us may be something like this. We are God's children, so we are simply loved. And that is grace. Grace is not earned, it is not accomplished or achieved. It is not extracted by manipulation or seduction. It is just given.

Graciousness

If grace comes from God's love for us, gracefulness or graciousness is how we express our receipt of that grace. Graciousness is kindness and mercifulness, an overflowing or an outpouring of God's grace through us. To say somebody is gracious is, I believe, one of the greatest compliments we can pay. 'Tá sí grástúil agus seolta,' my mother would say about a wonderful lady in the parish whom we all knew was saintly.

Grace is amazing

Countless attempts have been made to express the wonder of grace. One, by the nineteenth-century evangelist John Newton, was to become the most famous folk hymn of modern times, 'Amazing Grace':

> It is grace that brought me safe thus far
> And grace will lead me home.
> We've been there ten thousand years
> Bright shining as the sun.
> We've no less days to sing God's praise
> Than when we'd first begun.

Even with the best attempts of poets and artists to describe it, grace remains amazing. No words, parables, metaphors or artistic creations can do justice to its glory.

Grace in our ordinary lives

It is in our ordinary lives that we encounter God; it is in our ordinary lives that we express our graciousness, because it is in God that we 'live and move and have our being' (Acts 17:28).

No one of us could exist without God's sustaining, divine love. Divine love must be as near as the beat of our hearts. When we review ordinary life through the eyes of faith, every bush can be a burning bush, revealing the Lord's grace-full presence:

> Earth crammed with heaven, and every
>   common bush afire with God,
> but only he who sees takes off his shoes, the
>   rest sit round it and pluck blackberries.
> > (from *'Aurora Leigh'*
> > by Elizabeth Barrett Browning*)*

In other words, God reigns over all creation and can use every particle of created matter as a vehicle to embody and manifest his grace and graciousness, or as Gerard Manley Hopkins put it,

> The world is charged with the grandeur of
>   God
> It will flame out like shining from shook foil.
> > (from *'God's Grandeur'*)

To arrive at this grace-filled life, we must realise that the urgings of the human heart for it can only be satisfied by God, and that we must hand ourselves over to God. As St Augustine says, 'You have made us for yourself, Oh God, and our hearts will remain restless until we rest in you.' Yet we are meant to be with God, even now, at every moment in our lives. This is why Hopkins tells us to hand over our lives, with all their worries and struggles, with all their fragilities and openness, delights and beauty, to God's keeping, and to give it now:

> Deliver it, early now, long before death.
> Give beauty back
> Beauty, beauty, beauty back to
> God, beauty's self and beauty's giver.
> See not a hair is, not an eyelash, not the least
>   lash lost,
> Every hair is,
> Hair of the head is numbered.
>   (from 'The Leaden Echo and the Golden Echo')

The more conscious we are of our importance in God's sight, the more gracious we become.

'Living into grace'

Grace is only truly appreciated and expressed in the actual, immediate expression of real-life situations; it can only be lived into and lived out of.

Because grace is a pure gift, our most meaningful encounters with it will probably come at unintended times, when we are caught off guard, when our manipulative systems are at rest or otherwise occupied. And yet living into the mystery of grace doesn't simply happen. To encounter grace as a real gift, we need to be open to it, we must prepare ourselves to receive this gift.

The facts of grace

Being gracious or living into grace does not depend upon receptivity alone. It also requires an active attempt to live life in accord with the facts of grace, even when we do not sense them directly. The facts of grace are simple: grace always exists, it is always available, it is always good, it is always victorious.

Living into grace means taking risks

Living into grace or living a grace-filled life, a gracious life, means trying to act on the basis of these facts. I do not do very well at it. My life has given me plenty of real evidence for the facts of grace – they are certainly verified in my prayers – but whenever I try to live in accord with them, it seems to me that I am taking a risk. The risk, of course, is to my attachments. If I try to live a grace-filled life, then I will be relinquishing the gods I have made of my attachments. Graciousness threatens all my normalities. In defence, I am likely to try to distort what I know about the facts of grace, or forget them entirely. Thus I must make a conscious effort of will, I must struggle with myself, if I am going to act in accord with these facts.

Choosing to take risks

No matter how oppressed we may be, we always retain some capacity to choose. We can choose to risk ourselves to the goodness of God, or to continue to strive for our own autonomy, or to give in to the power that oppresses us. The choice is totally up to us. When we take risks, when we let the props go and give ourselves up to the struggle, God's grace is more radiant than at other times. Grace empowers us to choose rightly in what seems to be the most choiceless of situations, but it does not and will not determine that choice.

So while grace is a gift from God, the power of grace flows more fully when we choose to act in harmony with divine will. In practical terms, this means staying in a situation, being willing to confront it as it is, remaining responsible for the choice one makes in response to it, while at the same time turning to God's grace, protection and guidance as the ground for one's choices and behaviour.

Grace builds on nature

But spiritual maturity depends heavily on integral human development. This truth has long been captured in the scholastic adage that grace builds on nature. Healthy, sane personality development is the most fertile soil in which grace can take root and grow. Growth in grace and graciousness can best happen in situations that foster personal human growth. A modern paraphrase of 'grace builds on nature' could be 'God meets us where we are'.

Essential capacities for growing into grace

To become grace-filled or gracious people, I believe we need to cultivate some essential capacities that enable us to grow into grace: prayerfulness, acceptance, awareness, friendship, courage, gentleness and the ability to live with questions and ambiguity.

Prayerfulness

Prayer is one way of preparing ourselves to receive the gift of grace – just expressing our desire for grace, with no making of deals or marketing or manipulation. As a giver of grace, God deserves a straightforward request, and as children of God we have a right to make such requests.

Friendship

Friendship can be a very important source of divine grace, because intimate knowledge of a friend can reveal the face of God. To the Apostle Philip's request to see the Father, Jesus responded, 'To have seen me is to see the Father. So how can you say, "Let us see the Father?"' Enigmatic as it may sound, Jesus' response comes down to this – he can show us what God is only by the way he reflects God in his own humanity. He can reveal the face of God only by showing us his own face. We, too, can find God's revelation in others if we look for it, and God's grace in others, and God's graciousness in others.

The theologian Monica Hellwig summarises clearly the truth of how Jesus is the image of God in humanity, how God is to be encountered, experienced in and through others, and how intimate friendships which embody the love of Christ can be for us a kind of temple where we see the face of God – moments of grace and graciousness. Hellwig's insight is beautifully illustrated by a story of how two brothers' love for each other transformed their friendship into a temple where God's grace was made known. This is the story:

Time before time, when the world was young, two brothers shared a field and a mill, each night dividing evenly the grain they had grown together during the day. One brother lived alone; the other had a wife and a large family. Now the single brother thought to himself one day, it isn't really fair that we divide the grain evenly. I have only myself to care for, but my brother has children to feed. So each night, he secretly took some of his grain to his brother's granary, to see that he was never without.

But the married brother said to himself one day, it isn't really fair that we divide the grain evenly, because I have children to provide for me in my old age, but my brother has no one. What will he do when he is old? So every night he secretly took some of his grain to his brother's granary. As a result, both of them always found their supply of grain graciously and mysteriously replenished each morning.

Then one night, they met each other halfway between the two houses and suddenly realised what had been happening. They embraced each other in love.

The story is that God witnessed their meeting and proclaimed, 'This is a holy place, a place of love, and here it is that my temple shall be built', and so it was. The holy place where God is made known to people is a place where human beings discover each other in love. This story for me is a story about grace and graciousness.

Acceptance

Tillich links self-acceptance with faith. He defines faith as 'the courage to accept our acceptance, despite feelings of unacceptability'. This formation of faith comes only when a person is struck by God's grace:

> Grace strikes us when we are in great pain and restlessness, when year after year the longed-for perfection of life does not appear and the old compulsions reign within us as they have for decades, when despair destroys all joy and courage. At that moment, a shaft of light breaks into our darkness and it is as though a voice is saying 'You are accepted, you are accepted, accepted by that which is greater than you, and the name of which you do not know. Do not ask for the name now, perhaps you will find it later. Do not try to do anything now, perhaps later you will do much. Do not seek for anything, do not perform anything, do not intend anything, simply accept the fact that you are accepted.' When that happens to us, we experience grace.*

---

* Paul Tullich *The Courage to Be*, Yale University Press, UK 1997.

This identity conversion is a true gift – we cannot prepare ourselves to accept ourselves, we cannot force ourselves to accept ourselves, but sometimes it happens when we receive the power to say 'yes' to ourselves. Peace enters into us and makes us whole. Self-hatred and self-contempt disappear and the self is reunited with self. And yet that requires that we work on it – it doesn't simply happen just like that. We must prepare ourselves for the accepting of ourselves. But when it does happen, we can say that grace has come upon us.

Awareness

Self-acceptance is dependent on awareness. The more awareness we have, the more skilfully we can handle whatever arises. Awareness is by far the most essential and powerful resource we have for effective change and working with life's challenges. That is why the practice of mindful awareness is so important.

Awareness is much greater than knowledge or thought. It is an activity of our larger intelligence, which responds immediately to what is, before we draw on any concept to analyse or interpret it. Its main feature is clarity. Certain meditative traditions liken awareness to a mirror which reflects without bias. It has also been likened to a sun, which illumines whatever it shines upon. Awareness radiates a broad, diffuse light that can reveal what is going on in any situation, beyond any idea we have about it.

Another important feature of awareness is its fluidity. Like a zoom lens, it can move back from any state of mind or emotion we are caught in, so that we can gain a larger perspective on what is happening. We can also penetrate situations, zeroing in on their subtlest details.

The third characteristic of awareness is its stability and continuity. No matter how much our thoughts or emotions carry us away, at any moment we can always return to being present and simply noticing what is happening. No matter how difficult a situation may be, when we face it squarely, letting our awareness shine forth and clarify what is happening, we find our place; that is, we regain balance and confidence. When thoughts take control, they cause us to lose our place and feel disconnected. When we practise simple awareness, however, we can keep our place and go forth to meet what is in front of us in a saner way.

It can be difficult to achieve awareness, because we have an investment in maintaining and promoting an old, familiar version of reality. We are blinded by conditioned hopes and fears, by cherished perceptions, beliefs and opinions of all kinds, both personal and collective. We perpetuate these conditioned ways of perceiving the world, through repetitive stories we tell ourselves about the way things are. Usually we don't recognise these stories as our own invention; we believe they represent reality. Our entrenched perceptions and beliefs obscure the natural clarity and fluidity of awareness. We need to find ways of catching ourselves in the act of inventing these stories and return to the simple awareness of what is happening. There is a danger here of talking too much about things rather than experiencing them. Practising awareness is a slow process, and something we have to struggle to do every day.*

With greater consciousness, we can begin to dislodge the stories that control our behaviour, and thus develop greater clarity and freedom in our lives. In the Zen tradition, this is called polishing the mirror. Through this kind of practice, we can learn to feel more present to whatever is happening in our experience, as it is from moment to moment apart from our beliefs, judgements and fantasies about it. This helps us to connect with our own living wisdom and grace. Awareness can open us to grace, and grace-filled lives.

Courage

When we practise this awareness and acceptance, we also cultivate hope and courage. Once we start to develop a greater awareness, we grow in grace-fullness. But we might not like what we see; difficult feelings may arise; we may doubt that we can handle it; and so we may attempt to avert our gaze and fall back into unconsciousness.

It is not enough just to see what is happening; we must also be willing to extend ourselves to make a connection with it. This means opening ourselves to our experience and feeling it, facing it squarely and letting it affect us. Being people of

---

* For more about this idea, see *Awareness* by Anthony de Mello, New York, Doubleday & Co. 1978; or *The Miracles of Mindfulness* by Thich Nhat Hanh, Rider, London, 1989.

courage and hope does not mean that we will not feel afraid; rather it is the willingness to stay open to our fear and our rawness, without running away. To wake up and confront what is actually happening rather than just going along with old stories and reactions and patterns is an act of hope, an act of faith, an act of courage.

Courage appears when I am willing to sit at the edge of my pain and look at it face to face. We can learn to do the same with fear, anger, grief or any other state of mind. We can move out to the edge of the fear, take our seat there and enquire into it, instead of being controlled by our fear stories. The word 'courage' comes from *coeur*, the French word for 'heart': the essence of courage is being willing to feel our heart, even in situations which are difficult or painful. When we connect with our experience, we can cultivate our being, our ability to be in the present moment. This allows us to feel our heart, to be open to the other, to be gracious.

Gentleness

Another component of grace-fullness is gentleness. It is not enough to practise courage and faith and hope. We must also be able to remain fluid and flexible when we come up against obstacles, and to do this, we must be gentle with ourselves.

Cultivating gentleness with ourselves is essential for fostering inner growth and development. Real intimacy leads into unknown territory, and we find our way only through trial and error. As we leave behind old familiar ways of being, we move towards new states of balance. Falling into one extreme or another is unavoidable along the way. This is how we grow in grace, so we must give ourselves permission to go overboard sometimes. If we attack ourselves for going off course, we can't learn from our mistakes.

Practising gentleness does not mean always liking what we see or simply tolerating whatever goes on in our relationships. If we don't like our feelings, we can make room for our dislike as well. If we are angry about a situation, we can let our anger be there, too. Whatever arises, if we are gentle, we can learn to be with it and let it be as it is. When we open to our experience as it is, without imposing any blame or manipulation on it, we start to make friends with ourselves. Only then can our defensive structure begin to relax, clearing the way for a larger wisdom to shine through for ourselves and for others. Like acceptance, awareness, faith and hope, gentleness is necessary for graciousness. Graciousness holds no grudge or vice. Like the sun, it simply allows us to see what is.

Living with emptiness and ambiguities

Grace-fullness or graciousness is about what seems useless, a waste of time. It means moving into and surrendering to the deeper part of ourselves. Asian thinking expresses it like this: Quit trying, quit trying not to try, quit quitting. It means less preoccupation with doing things and more ability to let things happen; less attention to making decisions and more ability to letting things be; less reasoning and thinking, and more intuition; less focus on what I am unable to do, and more attention to and faith in the positive thing God is creating in my inner being; less anxiety about progress in prayer, in life or in action, and more reliance on God's action in me; less concern about the quality of my life and a deeper realisation that the authentic is found only in expressed love and concern for others; less searching for God and more awareness of all the places God finds us in our daily lives.

The important thing is that I surrender to this love and allow it to envelop my life. This means waiting, not being afraid of the dark, of the silence and of the emptiness. It is precisely in this emptiness, darkness and nothingness that grace is brought forth. This is the pregnancy that bears divine fruit. Meister Eckhart puts it this way:

> A man had a dream, a daydream. It seemed to him that he was big with nothingness, as a woman is with child. In this nothingness, God was born. He was the fruit of nothingness. God was born in nothingness.

Nobody sums it up better than T.S. Eliot in 'East Coker', *Four Quartets*:

> I said to my soul, be still and wait for God's rope
> The rope will be hope or the wrong thing
> Rage without love
> For love will be love for the wrong thing –
> there is yet fate
> But the faith and the love and the hope are
> all in the waiting
> Wait for that thought, for you are not ready
> for thought

So the darkness shall be the light and the
    stillness, the dancing
Whisper of running streams and winter
    lightning
The wild thyme unseen and the wild
    strawberry
The laughter in the garden – ecstasy
Not lost, but requiring pointing to the
    agony of death and birth.
They say I am repeating something I have
    said before
I shall say it again. Shall I say it again?
In order to arrive there, to arrive where you
    are, to get from where you are not, you
    must go the way wherein there is no
    ecstasy.
In order to arrive at what you do not know,
    you must go by a way which is the way
    of ignorance.
In order to possess what you do not
    possess, you must go by the way of
    dispossession.
In order to arrive at what you are not, you
    must go through the way in which you
    are not.
And what you do not know is the only
    thing you know.
What you own is what you do not own, and
    where you are is where you are not.

The possibilities within

These are the basics of grace-filled lives. Whatever
our habitual tendencies to fight or flee when we

come up against painful or difficult situations, they allow us to convert whatever challenges us. And most of us carry these possibilities within us. Our relationships provide many hard surfaces on which to sharpen these abilities, and the sharper they become, the further we can advance along the path.

The universe is gratis

Yet no matter how much we try to be open and receptive to grace, we must never forget that grace still remains a pure gift from God. 'The universe may be as great as they say, but it wouldn't be missed if I didn't exist.' With a disarming smile, this little jingle by Piet Hein lays bare the gratuitousness of absolutely everything. The universe is gratis, it cannot be earned, nor need it be earned, and the simple fact of experience brings grace-filled living. Graciousness is a heart's full response to the gratuitousness of all that exists. Graciously, we open ourselves to this gracious universe and so become fully graced with it. In doing so, we learn to move gracefully with its loads, as in a universal dance.

Walking with grace-fullness

There are no facile methods or gurus that can tell us ahead of time how to walk with grace-fullness in all the different situations we encounter. Throughout our lives, tension will accompany our efforts to be gracious in a balanced and harmonious way. A grace-filled Christian spirituality calls for the individual to be faithful to the struggle of loving, to be open to change and to trust that the guidance of the ever-present spirit of love is more important than fixed rules and techniques. True grace-fullness and graciousness consist in walking in the light of the spirit.

Guidelines

1: Prayer

Place yourself in God's presence

2: Breath prayer

| Breathe in: | Gracious God |
| Breathe out: | Envelop me |

3: Reading

Read a passage from Chapter 3.

4: Scripture

Col. 1: 24-29	'The mystery is Christ among you.'
1 Cor. 2: 10-16	'But we are those who have the mind of Christ.'
Eph. 2: 1-10	'We are God's work of art, created in Christ Jesus to live the good life.'

Let these words, phrases, scripture passages, stay with you.

Let them draw you into them.
Allow an image to emerge.
Listen to the image.
Talk to the image.

5: Images of graciousness

Questions which you may find helpful to evolve images:

- What image of graciousness most relates to your experience of graciousness?
- Do you have other images of graciousness that speak to you?
- Can you image it?
- What keeps you from being gracious?
- Can you image it?
- Is there a human image that evokes graciousness in you?
- Is there an image from art, in any of its forms, that brings you a sense of graciousness?
- Is there an image from nature that evokes a sense of graciousness?
- What beautiful things in life evoke graciousness in you?
- Can you image them?

Allow the image to the surface.
Allow it come into your awareness.
Stay with it.
Listen to it.
Talk to it.

6: The journal

The following questions may help with your writing:

- If someone were to say to you 'What do you understand by graciousness', what would you say, what would you reply?
- What are the things or people that evoke graciousness in you?
- What keeps you from being gracious?
- When you feel you are losing your graciousness what helps you restore it?
- Can you remember a special time in your life when you experienced graciousness in a particular radiant way?
- Was it a person? an experience? was it God?
- Have you a memory of a person who radiates graciousness?

7: Thanks

Give thanks to our gracious God and ask for a gracious heart.

Chapter 2

Hope

I spent a few days this summer in rural Ireland. Walking in nature, I was awakened again to my childhood, where I was surrounded by the silent activity of the garden and the fields, the slow unfolding of buds, the unseen ripening of potatoes, the fullness of the corn fields and the bounty of the apple trees. At harvest-time, that silence was replaced by the activity of the threshing, the gathering of fruits, the stacking of hay, the cutting of turf. The hopes of the planting season had been fulfilled; the long process of waiting had ended. As I walked the beaches of my home area, swam in the sea or went fishing, I found myself in touch with the steadfast rhythms of the ocean – another opportunity to be stretched by the magnificence and power of creation, and be calmed and strengthened and restored and delighted in every part of my being.

Hope in spite of pain

And yet I know that in human terms the growth and the harvest and the steadfastness and the peace are less clear. The groping, searching, waiting, gathering follow no sure pattern and have no sure outcomes. Food and clothes don't reach those most in need. Homes are not available to many people who are homeless. Friends are dying of lung cancer and of AIDS. Others are fighting their addictions and against prejudices. Innocent children are the pawns of people with power over them. The agony of the world is written in the human faces that I meet every day. And as hope dawns on one part of our world, shadow covers another. And yet, even here, in the fragile people all around me, who start each day afresh, who are sick, have disabilities, are out of work, out of home, here there is still hope, here there are people who in spite of terrible experiences are able to be strong and are able to be a source of hope to others.

Losing touch, losing hope

It is easy to lose hope when we lose touch with our sources. We can walk amidst nature's beauty and talk non-stop, without stopping to see. We can become immune to the grandeur and the glory of creation. I have spent days and weeks when I didn't notice a cloud passing over the moon or the dew drops clinging to the leaves or the blackberries or the robin. We avoid the heat and the cold, we screen our windows against the winter, fence off our gardens and eliminate weeds, even though they too, like garden plants, have names and blossoms. We protect ourselves from nature; we get accustomed to eating consumer food products without a thought for where they grew or where they came from. It is easy to get trapped in a hectic mechanical lifestyle, getting up to the sound of an alarm clock, battered by news from the radio, tested by traffic, forced to calculate time and distance to the second, going through the day using phones and lifts and gadgets, and then home again at the end of the day, through more traffic, with more news being shouted at us.

It is easy to allow routines, the ticking of the clock, daily trivia to rule our lives. It is only when we bend our head in prayer that we give ourselves a chance to remember that we are all on a journey, we are pilgrims, nomads, in exodus, that we have the seed of God in us, and that, as Meister Eckhardt says, 'The seed of God grows into God as a hazel seed grows into a hazel tree.' It is because that seed of God is within us, wanting to grow in us, that we can't settle, we can't let ourselves become too complacent.

Our capacity for hope can diminish when there is no room for miracle or mystery. Our pragmatic mindsets can become convinced that most of the situations we find ourselves in are humanly solvable problems, problems of racism, of urban decay, of crime, of mental illness, domestic and personal problems, problems of homelessness or poverty or unemployment, even problems of inter-church dialogue. In this kind of atmosphere there is no room for hope, because hope belongs to the realm of the ongoing mystery, the human endeavour to penetrate the darkness and the obscurity of the realities that surround us. Love and truth, suffering and death are realities that we are involved in, not objective problems we confront. We are developed by them as we experience them; we are in them, not outside them; they transcend us and compel us to explore a larger world of interaction and exchange. And that is what we are called to as Christians. That is the Good News. Our lives are not trivia or defined by the problems we face. We are marked by freedom. As St Paul said, 'You are a letter of Christ, written not in ink but in the spirit of the living God.'

We are called to hope

We are summoned as Christians to a bold commitment to act in faith. It is no trivial task, to give an account of the hope that is in us in the midst of overwhelming poverty, in the face of sickness, through grief and insult and loneliness, speaking forcefully and without malice, restructuring our priorities and making credible our value systems, plodding patiently through daily tasks and commitment. The call to release life and meaning from all the secret and dim events of our personal and communal histories is our challenge as Christians. We are called to probe the forbidden, to unmask monsters, to look death in the eye; we are called to love in love's inimitable way by service and sacrifice and substitution. Our spirits may be weak, our bodies tired, but we hunger still for good news, and in that lies our hope.

St Augustine says that hope has two daughters, anger and courage. It is they who enable us to make happen what we want to happen in the future. They enable us to do remarkable things; they lead us to treat as our brothers and sisters the rejected people of the world, the homeless people, the unemployed, the people living with AIDS, the men and women in jails; they lead us to beg bread at the communal table of our churches; they lead us to turn upside down the hierarchical system, the male-dominated structures, the class-conscious conventions, the mindsets, the success syndromes; and they lead us to transform by tiny deliberate efforts the priorities and preoccupations of our personal lives and to believe in the transformation of society, even while nothing seems to improve or change.

Hope lives on the edge

My father used to say to us, 'Tóg go bog é agus bogfaidh sé chughat' – take it easy, and it will ease with you. And my mother would say, 'Fan agus cífidh tú'. She wasn't just saying 'Wait and see' she was saying 'If you trust, you will see; it will happen; this too will pass'. Hope lives on the edge between the near and the far, the finite and the infinite, the now and the not yet. It is believing what is not yet seen, and seeing what is not yet visible, or as Dan Berrigan puts it, 'living as though the truth were true'. It is when we are told the limits of our life that we hope.

Guidelines

1: Prayer

Place yourself in God's presence.

2: Breath prayer

Breathe in: Spirit of hope
Breathe out: Encourage me

3: Reading

Read a passage from chapter 2.

4: Scripture

Dt 31: 1-8	'Be strong stand firm for Yahweh Your God is going with you.'
Rom 8: 31-39	'With God on our side, who can be against us?'
Jn 14: 1-7	'Do not let your hearts be troubled.'

Let these words, phrases, scripture passages, stay with you.
Let them draw you into them.
Allow an image to emerge.
Listen to the image.
Talk to the image.

5: *Images of hope*

Questions which you may find helpful to evolve images:

- What image of hope most relates to your experience of hope?
- Do you have other images of hope that speak to you?
- What image of hope do you bring to the world?
- What image of hope does your world bring to you?
- What gives you hope in hard times? Can you image it?
- Is there an image from music that brings hope to your heart?
- Is there an image from art, in any of its forms, that brings you a sense of hope?
- Is there an image from nature that evokes hope in you?
- What beautiful things in life evoke hope in you?
- Can you image them?

Allow the image to the surface.
Allow it to come into your awareness.
Stay with it.
Listen to it.
Talk to it.

6: *The journal*

The following questions may help with your writing:

- If someone were to say to you – 'What do you understand by hope?' what would you say, what would you reply?

- What are the hopes that encourage you now?
- What keeps you from having hope?
- What happens to you when you feel you are losing hope?
- What happens when you feel you have lost hope?
- How can you restore your hope?
- Remember a time in your life when your hope was restored.
- What or who is it that gives you hope?
- Is it a person? Is it a purpose? Is it a past experience? Or is it your faith in God?
- What does it mean to belong to the God of hope?
- How has God given you hope?
- Name the unhopeful aspects of your life.
- What hope has God given you this week?
- Where and to whom do you really want to bring hope?
- How can you do that?

7: Thanks

Give thanks to God, the giver of hope, and ask for a deepening of your hope.

Chapter 3

Solidarity

'The joy, the hope, the grief and the anguish of the people of our time, especially those who are poor and afflicted, are the joy, the hope, the grief and the anguish of the followers of Christ as well.' These words, from the Second Vatican Council, echo the words of Christ himself. It was Jesus who invited us to walk with the poor.

To be in solidarity with someone means to 'stand solidly with' them. The one thing Jesus asked us to do was to love, and that's the one thing we have great difficulty in doing. He invited us to enter into a covenant with him and with our brothers and sisters, especially the poorest and most rejected ones, a covenant of solidarity. In order to be in solidarity with the poor, we must try to understand the life of the poor in a very deep way; to love in a very deep way; to accept their situation as it really is; and to struggle all the time to understand better the structures that oppress them. It is not enough to feel sorry for the poor; we have to stand with them and learn from them. In her poem, 'Some People' Rita Ann Higgins writes:

Some people know what it is like ...
to be second hand
to be second class
to be no class
to be looked down on
to be walked on
to be pissed on
to be shat on
and other people don't.

(from *Goddess and Witch*,
Salmon Publishing 1988)

Clearly some people know, and some people don't know, what it is to be poor.

Solidarity is a struggle

For those of us who are not poor, it is a daily struggle to stand in solidarity with the poor. In order to walk with and be on the side of the poor, we must try to accept their situation as it really is and understand the structures of society that oppress them.

In order to come to some understanding of what it is like to be poor, we have to be taught by the poor, and to be taught by the poor is to be taught in a totally different way from the way we are used to being taught. Being taught by the poor is not about doing, achieving, having answers; it is really about discovering our true selves.

The story of Bartimaeus

One poor person we can learn from is Bartimaeus, the blind beggar of the gospel story:

> And they reached Jericho, and as he left Jericho with his disciples and a large crowd, Bartimaeus, that is the son of Timaeus, a blind beggar, was sitting at the side of the road. When he heard it was Jesus of Nazareth, he began to shout and say, 'Son of David, Jesus, have pity on me!' and many of them scolded him, and told him to be quiet, but he only shouted all the louder, 'Son of David, have pity on me!' Jesus stopped and said, 'Call him here.' So they called the blind man. 'Courage,' they said. 'Get up, he's calling you.' So, tearing off his cloak, he jumped up and went to Jesus. Then Jesus spoke. 'What do you want me to do for you?' The blind man said to him, 'Master, let me see again.' And Jesus said to him, 'Go, your faith has saved you,' and immediately his sight returned and he followed him along the road.

Jesus was just leaving Jericho, on his way to Jerusalem. He was followed by a huge crowd, and 'at the side,' or on the margins, this blind beggar was sitting. He heard (because he couldn't see) that Jesus of Nazareth was passing by, and he shouted, 'Son of David, Jesus, have pity on me!' And the crowd scolded him to be quiet: he was interrupting, did he not know that Jesus was here? The crowd told him to be quiet, 'stay in your place,' like what you would say to a dog.

Maybe they didn't mean to be harsh. The blind man at the edge, he couldn't see, so he was shouting. We can all get irritated with somebody who goes prattling on or interrupts when we are doing something important, preparing to meet an important person perhaps. It might be a mentally handicapped person, a deaf person who shouts, an old person who is not tuned in; but in any case, they are getting in the way, interrupting our train of thought, distracting people. But getting irritated with people who interrupt like this, telling them to be quiet – that is not standing in solidarity with them, in their joy, in their grief, in their anguish, that is not honouring the covenant we have made with them. The people in the crowd wanted Bartimaeus to be quiet out of deference to Jesus. There was somebody special here, somebody sacred, and they wanted to concentrate on that. But the point that they missed was that Bartimaeus, the blind beggar, was sacred too, as we all are, each and every one. We all have a right to be heard, we all have a right not to be excluded and pushed to the margins.

Crowds

We have all been in crowds and we have been bullied by the organisers of the crowd – for example there were huge crowds here in Ireland at the Phoenix Park, in Galway, at Knock or wherever, at the time of the Pope's visit. We were put into corrals, and there were fellows in caps with newly found power for the day, pushing us around. That wasn't a very pleasant experience, being put in a box and not being able to move out of it. Some people like to manipulate situations like that, to use their influence to get into a better position within the crowd. But, like blind Bartimaeus, the poor can never do that, for every time they try, they are put back in their box, they are put back on the side of the crowd, on the margins of society.

Crowds, as we know, are fickle. When Jesus heard the blind man, he said 'Call him here.' Immediately the crowd changed its tune. They said, 'Courage, get up! He's calling you!' The blind beggar was important now, all of a sudden, because Jesus was calling him. Fickleness is not an attribute of solidarity. If we want to be in solidarity with the poor, we need to be prepared to accept them, whatever their story. We shouldn't make exceptions or change our tune when we hear someone say, That's the daughter or son of so-and-so, but they fell on bad times and happened to get on drugs.

Blessed are the poor

Jesus didn't behave like that. He noticed, he paid attention, he listened with his heart; he was in no hurry. He was prepared to depart from his agenda, as the Good Samaritan departed from his. Jesus was concerned with what was important more than with what was urgent. Jesus was tuned in to the poor. 'Blessed are the poor,' Jesus said. He didn't say what we might like him to have said: 'Blessed are those who are getting on in life,' or 'Blessed are those who get things done,' or 'Blessed are those who understand.' He said 'Blessed are the poor,' and that is what he meant. He meant that the truculent, the slow, the ones that don't turn up, the ones that mess up things, the ones that cause trouble, the ones that interrupt and make a fuss are blessed. The poor are blessed, the ones we like and the ones we don't like too.

Here in this gospel story we see him putting that principle into action, stopping to attend to the needs of the poor blind beggar. With no ambiguity, very gently, he beckoned the man to come. He was in touch, in the deepest way, with this blind beggar. And then he spoke those beautiful words, some of the most beautiful words in the Gospel, 'What do you want me to do for you?' When the blind man said, 'Master, let me see again,' Jesus said to him, 'Go, your faith has saved you,' and immediately his sight returned and he followed Jesus along the road. Jesus looked into this man's eyes, he restored not only his sight, but he restored his dignity and his pride; he gave him a place; he made him feel significant.

Going against the crowd

Jesus was fearless in doing this. He went against the crowd. He called up the disturber, the man who was told to get into his place, and when they saw what Jesus did, the crowd changed. Jesus knew exactly what he was doing. There are moments when we too are under the gaze of all and we encounter a poor person, outside the church, maybe, or on the street. This can make us feel awkward or ill at ease, but if we want to be in solidarity with the poor, we need to learn how to be with people in situations like that. This doesn't mean that we have to give all the time to people who approach us, but we need to learn to be with them, to look them in the eye, to treat them as friends. And they know if we are with them.

Learning from the poor

If we feel a distance from the poor, maybe it is because we have our own agenda. Maybe we are not able to be with people, but are always looking instead to see what we can do. Most of us were brought up that way, always wanting to be doing things, looking for success, looking for control, wanting to know the right people. It is a daily struggle for each of us to unlearn those values and to recondition ourselves. Of course, some people are gifted by God to be great doers, great achievers, great organisers, but to learn that these are not the only gifts we are given by God is a life-long struggle. And we can learn this from the poor because they are not interested in competition, they are not interested in who people know, this does not impress them.

Discovering our true selves

The poor challenge us to pray daily to discover our true selves, to discover more and more the common humanity we share with all. They challenge us to go on this journey, which is a very painful journey, questioning our values, striving to be our true selves, striving to be at one with ourselves and at one with all.

Jesus' solidarity

It is a painful, confusing process. We are afraid of losing our identity, an identity that we have worked to achieve, and this pain, this fear can be very real. The poor challenge us to accept who we are – not what we can do, not what we possess, not what we have done. They challenge us to live more simply. A central question for us as Christians is whether we are open enough to allow the poor to change us, or do I want to change them?

It is very hard to learn the lessons of the poor if our gifts are constantly being rewarded, our ability to do, to organise, to achieve is being approved and applauded. This is a great lesson the poor can teach us. Bartimaeus has a lot to teach us. He has a lot of energy. He stands up, drops everything, runs to Jesus. He didn't stop to ask, What will people think of me? What will happen to me? What will be asked of me? He didn't have the baggage that the rest of us carry and that comes in our way when we meet Jesus, or when we meet the poor. Jesus recognised the fearlessness of the blind man. It was as if he was linked directly with the blind man. And this is solidarity.

Jesus' style wasn't cramped by the crowd – it was never cramped. It wasn't cramped by the Pharisees, by the important people. Jesus' mission was very clear – he came to the lost sheep of the house of Israel, and nobody or nothing would deflect him, seduce him, manipulate or blind him in any way from that mission. This is amazing! We could meditate on this all our lives. He simply knew his mission, and though the Pharisees corrected him for healing the sick on the Sabbath day, for not washing his hands before eating, for picking the corn, Jesus spoke out harshly against them. He said, 'You honour me with your lips, but your heart is far from me.' He said, 'You brood of vipers, you whited sepulchres, you are all white on the outside but inside you are full of rotten bones.' Jesus was always true, always congruent.

Now he looks at the crowd, the crowd is sickening, the crowd is weak, the crowd is fainthearted. Nothing disappoints Jesus more than our faintheartedness, our apathy. 'I wish you were hot or cold, but because you are lukewarm,' Jesus said, 'I want to vomit you out of my mouth.' Nothing fainthearted about Jesus; nothing fainthearted about the blind man. The blind man said, 'I want to see again.' He hadn't the slightest doubt or the slightest hesitation. This was his deepest desire. And Jesus looked at him and he knew what was in his heart and he said, 'Your faith has saved you.' And immediately the blind man's sight was restored and he stood up, and he followed Jesus along the road. He didn't get the gift for himself, he got it to share.

Our deepest desire

What if Jesus stood in front of us? Are we ready for the miracle, even a miracle we don't understand? Are we ready to be changed utterly, transformed utterly? What is our deepest desire? Is it on the tip of our tongue or jumping out of our heart, or is it silenced by our baggage? When we pray, 'Thy kingdom come,' what are we praying for? Is it for the kingdom of peace and love and joy and simplicity and gentleness and righteousness in our heart, in our family, in our community, or is it for the kingdom of changing the system so that the poor can be free and like us? 'What do you want me to do for you?' Jesus is waiting for us to discover our deepest desire.

This is our deepest desire – to know that we are loved, that we are loved absolutely and totally and unconditionally, so that through that love we too will be able to love unconditionally, gratefully and joyfully, be able to receive love, to go out to others and make sacrifices for others. Jesus is waiting to give us this gift of love, the gift of our true selves, who are made in the image of God, reaching out to the poorest and the weakest, as Jesus did.

But our deepest desire is often covered over by things, by other values, by false gods, and this is how the poor can help us. They can help us to see where we are not committed, to see where we come and go without a commitment, to see what parts of us are not yet transformed. If we listen, they will help us to discover our blind spots, and we can stand before Jesus, and hear him say, 'What do you want, because I want to give it to you, because you are my beloved child.' Jesus only wants to give us what is good, he only wants to give us love, he only wants to enable us to love. If we believe that, then we will go with it, we won't worry. We won't worry what people will think, we won't mind them, we won't mind what 'the men on Brady's Hill will say'. That's the great gift of the poor – the gift of showing us our blind spots so that we can be more open. If we allow the poor to release to us our full self, in our brokenness, in our blindness, then when that is revealed to us, we can stand before God and know what we want healed, know what we want of him. When he asks us, 'What do you want me to do for you?' we will know the answer. And if we are open to his ability to change us, we can make 'the joy, the hope, the grief, the anguish of the people of our times, especially those who are poor and afflicted, our joy, our hope, our grief, our anguish,' just as Jesus did.

Guidelines

1: prayer

Place yourself in God's presence

2: Breath prayer

Breathe in: Lover of the outcast
Breathe out: Give me your love

3: Reading

Read passage from Chapter 4.

4: Scripture

Mt 5: 3-9	The Beatitudes
Lk 10: 29-37	The Good Samaritan
Mt 10: 46-52	The Story of Bartimaeus

Let these words, phrases, scripture passages, stay with you.
Let them draw you into them.
Allow an image to emerge.
Listen to the image.
Talk to the image.

5: Images of solidarity

Questions which you may find helpful to evolve images:

- What image of solidarity most relates to your experience of standing solidly with the poor?
- Do you have other images of solidarity that speak to you?
- What image do you have of an excluded person, a marginalised person?
- What image do you have of the poor being our teachers?

Maybe you would like to form an image from the scene at the outskirts of Jericho, as described in Matthew chapter 10. Put yourself into that crowd. Look at the different characters in the crowd. Where are you in the crowd? Are you in the front? the back? the middle? or hidden? Who do you identify with in the crowd?

Look at Bartimaeus, the blind beggar. And look at Jesus. And look at the crowds scolding the blind man for interrupting Jesus. Who are you in that story? Are you the blind beggar? Are you the people in the crowd that are trying to keep him back? Are you the disciples of Jesus who are trying to make way for Jesus, without noticing? Or are you Jesus who notices everyone, particularly the weakest and the most excluded? Or are you Bartimaeus who stopped the crowd in their tracks?

- Have you discovered a Bartimaeus in your life?
- If you have, how has this person or persons affected you?
- What have they taught you?
- What could help you to listen to Bartimaeus?
- What is it in your life that prevents you from noticing Bartimaeus?
- Is there an image from music that brings solidarity to your heart?
- Is there an image from art, in any of its forms, that brings a sense of unity to you?
- Is there an image from nature that evokes in you solidarity?
- What beautiful things in life evoke in you a sense of solidarity?

Allow the image to surface.
Allow it to come into your awareness
Stay with it.
Listen to it.
Talk to it.

6: The journal

The following questions may help with your writing
- If someone were to ask you 'What do you understand by solidarity with the poor? what would you say?'
- What are the experiences of standing in solidarity with the poor that encourage you?

- What people give you a sense of solidarity?
- What people inspire you to stand in solidarity with the poor?
- What things help you to have the courage to stand in solidarity?
- What keeps you from living in solidarity with the poor?
- What do you fear about living in solidarity with the poor?
- What are your hopes about living in solidarity with the poor?
- Bartimaeus knew exactly what he wanted when Jesus asked him 'What do you want me to do for you?' If Jesus asked you what you wanted him to do for you, would you know what to say? Are you ready to answer?
- Are you ready to be transformed utterly, like the blind beggar?
- Are you ready to hear the good news and then to spread it?
- Why do you think you are so concerned about what people will say if you identify with the poor?
- Why do you give so much attention to what the 'men on Brady's Hill' will say?
- What would help you to be able to stand in solidarity with the poor? A person, an experience, an opportunity, faith, God?

7: Thanks

Give thanks to God and ask for the grace to live in greater solidarity with the poor.

Chapter 4

Celebration

Celebrating on occasions

I had a phone call recently from someone who worked with us in Focus some years ago. She was talking about her time with us and she mentioned in particular how much she had enjoyed the way we used to celebrate everything.

It is true that we have a strong tradition in Focus of celebrating regularly and frequently. We celebrate at the beginning of each year and at the end of each year. We celebrate when people came to work with us, and when they leave. We celebrate the birthday of Focus itself and we celebrate each other's birthdays.

Part of the reason we have such a strong commitment to celebration in Focus is that I brought that tradition with me from two sources: from my own childhood and from my days working with Bishop Birch in Kilkenny Social Services. My childhood was spent on the Dingle peninsula in the forties and fifties. We celebrated on all sorts of occasions: marriages, baptisms, wakes, stations, harvest, people returning from abroad. We celebrated the seasons: when the cutting and footing and bringing home of the turf was complete and the harvest was done, the people gathered together for the threshing and the putting away of the turf for the winter. At the stations, a lovely tradition carried over from Penal times, each household in turn celebrated spiritually and socially with their neighbours; first we had a Eucharist and sacrament of reconciliation, and afterwards there were food and drink and festivities that went on until the small hours. When people left to go to America, there was a community goodbye, and when the emigrants returned home, there was great jubilation. The local community hosted a Ball Night, which went on right through the night. In brief, the neighbourhood celebrated each other. We lived, as Peig Sayers said, in each other's shadow: 'Is ar scath a chéile a mhaireann na daoine.'

When I was working with Bishop Birch in Kilkenny in the sixties and seventies, I learned a lot about celebration. Any occasion was an opportunity to celebrate. Our celebrations were inclusive: we included the spiritual and the secular, the rich and the poor, the clergy and the laity, the settled and the unsettled.

I was at a wedding recently which was a truly wonderful celebration, so beautifully done, the flowers, the colours, everything carefully planned with attention to the likes and preferences of the people being married, a loving, gentle and simple celebration of the joy of the couple. The bride was a wheelchair-user, and many of the guests also had disabilities. People with disabilities are often prevented from participating fully in our society, and perhaps that is why when they celebrate, it is with a special joy. Clearly visible were the honour and love the couple had for each other and the extraordinary outpouring of heartfelt joy as people celebrated together and celebrated each other.

Celebrating the person

We celebrate on particular occasions, as the Dingle people did at harvest or at a homecoming, as people working in Focus do on a birthday, as we did in Kilkenny if somebody did well at an exam, for example, as the people did at the wedding, but the occasion is not really the point. What we are doing on these occasions is celebrating each other and our living and working together. The purpose of celebration is not to prove anything. It is simply to express our care for each other, our union with each other, and at the same time it forges a deeper union.

Going to a party is not the same as celebrating, or at least it is not the same as celebrating a person. When we are celebrating a person we have to become involved, we have to give some thought to the form the celebration will take so that it is appropriate for the person; we have to try to make it special for them; we have to take part in the preparations, making arrangements about music, flowers and so forth. Finding a gift for a person on their birthday, for their wedding or when they are about to leave us is also a very important part of celebration. It need not be expensive but it should symbolise and reflect the person's preferences, their specialness and their preciousness. Sometimes today people expect that celebrations should be spontaneous, and it is good if we are close enough to our friends to be able to celebrate with them spontaneously, but we also need planned celebrations, where the care we take with the planning is itself part of honouring and celebrating the person.

Celebrating each other

Because of these two events – the phone call from my old colleague and the wedding – I began to reflect on the meaning of celebration and the place it should have in our lives. True celebration is always about people. It is honouring and celebrating each other. As we celebrate each other, we carry each other, as a mother carries her child. We carry each other by being present to each other, by a steady flow of encouragement and acceptance, by our willing participation in each other's lives and burdens, by placing ourselves in each other's place and living each other's experience, by taking pride in each other's fruitfulness and taking joy in each other's joy.

Celebration of each other means recognising that everyone needs to be appreciated. We are all spiritual beings, which means that there is a deep alive place within each of us that longs for fulfilment. There are qualities within ourselves and within others of which we are not aware until we are willing to venture beyond our own comfort zone and enter into the lives of others.

Competition and fear: the opposites of celebration and love

We live in a society that tells us that if we are successful we will be rewarded and we can *only* be successful if we work hard and get to the top. If we want to keep climbing, soon a 40-hour week becomes a 50-hour week and then a 60-hour week. This drive for success is the opposite of celebrating people; instead it makes people unhealthy and dispirited. This way of life does not lead to happiness; it is self-destructive. Most of us know how easily we can be seduced into that way of life. People who are caught up in this drive for success grab whatever they can to bolster themselves, and collude in a way of life that eventually results in a society dominated by greed and self-interest.

This way of life thrives on fear – fear of failure, fear of losing our individuality, fear of giving up something of ourselves, fear of not being in control and especially fear of love itself (which is the opposite of fear), fear of being opened by the force and call of love, of entering into reciprocity. Behind our every failure to love is the conviction that it is not safe to give ourselves spontaneously to life, to another person, to a group. We fear being changed, and at the end of this fear is complete isolation and loneliness; whereas at the end of love is celebration, community, conversion and on-going transformation.

Daring to take risks

But loving and celebrating the other presuppose risk. To love is to be vulnerable. C.S. Lewis says 'If you give your heart to no one it will become unbreakable, impenetrable, irredeemable' (from *Four Loves*, New York: Harcourt Brace 1960, pages 111-112); whereas giving your heart to someone ensures it will be broken, pierced, wounded and made malleable. It is when we acknowledge our brokenness and our weaknesses that we begin to accept ourselves as we really are and we move towards becoming more whole.

The psychologist Abraham Maslow once explained that in our western culture we are taught not to trust ourselves, not to trust what we know about our deepest desires and how to resolve our inner conflicts. We have been taught that behind the veneer of our social selves there lie repressed hostilities and other evils and we have been taught not to risk exploring that unconscious part of our mind. And yet it is precisely by entering into the recesses of our hearts, following our deepest desires, that we can become whole. That is the risk we take together in loving environments when we acknowledge each other as people and encourage each other to choose living life to the full and to choose knowing ourselves.

Recognising our own weakness and vulnerability

Three thousand years ago the *I Ching* (the Chinese book of philosophy) explained that once an individual has looked honestly into his own heart he will never fear any threat that comes from outside himself. That insight holds the key to all our lives. The door it unlocks is to a humility that seems the very antithesis of our contemporary understanding of ambition and success.

Bergman's film *Face to Face* tells the story of Jenny, a psychiatrist who has managed her life with almost total professional control. When confronted with lack of control and painful wisdom in a psychotic patient, Jenny faces herself in a kind of distorted mirror. Her patient Maria tells her: 'You are unable to love. You are almost unreal. I have tried to like you as you are, because I thought, then she will become more real, less anxious and more sure of herself, but not a hope! Jenny looks at me with her lovely big blue eyes, the most beautiful eyes in the world and all I see is her anguish. Have you ever loved anybody Jenny?'

This insight of Maria's brings about Jenny's own breakdown and causes her to recognise the emptiness of her life. She recognises that she needs to live with greater authenticity and integrity as a person, not in the empty role of a professional woman. What Jenny discovered was what she had in common with her patient – a shared suffering, which she had denied to herself up to this point.

Celebration in loving community

The first time I saw that film, I realised in a very vivid and profound way that the same thing can happen to any of us, when we are prepared to face ourselves and our own vulnerability; but that is not easy. It is difficult to take the risks that love demands of us; it is difficult to reveal our vulnerability. And that is why living and working in a caring, celebratory community that is prepared to take those risks can be an enormous support. In a loving environment where we celebrate each other, we enter into the mystery of love and exchange deep love where no-one who comes to us will be rejected.

For some time now I have been living as part of a small community that is part of Focus. We all come with different personalities, temperaments, backgrounds and traditions and when we live closely as a small community all our hurts and brokenness and joys and fears and struggles and hopes are exposed. It is not an easy thing to face those parts of ourselves. It is easier to avoid them. But when we face our inner selves, then we really become more reconciled within ourselves and also realise how much people love us, even in our brokenness.

Living in a loving community doesn't have to mean living in a religious community. It can be any caring environment – a family, a neighbourhood, a group of people who work together or any group that comes together for the benefit of all its members. In a community or caring environment, we celebrate ourselves with all our weaknesses, our faults and failings. The environment of love always opens up new gifts. Gifts that were not evident before become evident and can be channelled in new directions. Gifts only partly known by certain people can be nurtured and expanded in a loving environment. Other gifts can be called forth from people who never knew they had them. Some of those elicited gifts are buried in the past, because they didn't seem to count.

When we live close to one another in community or in a loving environment, it is hard not to know everything that is wrong with each other, including the failings and the mistakes of the past. With this awareness there comes a choice: we can complain about and judge the other person or we can love them. The only thing greater than our awareness is love and the awareness of God's love for us and God's desire to see us healed and made whole.

Loving environments – whether we live our lives in communities, groups or families – are about love and mutual trust. In loving environments, people enjoy being together and working together towards the same goal. It is not always easy, but the community binds together in a mysterious way the pain and the joy of its people. Every one of us is deeply vulnerable, and in our hearts we have a deep longing to love and be loved, a longing for tenderness and compassion and understanding in our personal relationships; but we also experience our wounds, our guilts, our fears, and these can cause divisions and blocks that cut people off from each other. Sometimes our woundedness can lead to divisions and the tearing apart of a community, or it can manifest itself by hiding from each other and being simply polite to each other – but the wounds are still there. It is only when we accept each other with an open heart and celebrate each other that we can acknowledge our woundedness and our brokenness.

One of the great lessons of living in a community or place of celebration is that we know that God breaks into the part of us that is weak. God's spirit is active in the most unlikely of places, in the poor and the broken, and in humble places the power of God is most realised, at the point of vulnerability, of risk-taking or letting go. To be vulnerable means to be available to the power of God and celebratory communities bring us to the point where God's love can break in.

Some people seem to think that a community is for those who cannot support themselves, and of course we have our weaknesses in communities and people who feel weak and vulnerable need community. But I often think that people in our society who consider themselves strong and whole by the world's standards need a community or people around them even more. There are persons who can experience the deepest conversion and reconciliation in community, because for the first time their weak places are acknowledged and accepted, their whole person is celebrated, they need not hide nor fear their insecure place, no longer do they have to foster and play to their strengths. They can be accepted and loved in the wholeness that is strength and weakness.

Celebration is about reconciliation

Celebration implies forgiveness and flows from it. When the prodigal son returned home after his life away, his father forgave him and gathered everyone around for a feast. He said to his servants 'Hurry! Bring the most beautiful robe and put it on him, put a ring on his finger and shoes on his feet. Bring the fatted calf and kill it. We will eat and celebrate, as a son who was dead has returned to life, he was lost and he is found and we will celebrate together.'

Not only was the prodigal son forgiven, but he was celebrated. Of course it is not always easy. The embrace of the forgiving father healed the wounded and humiliated heart of the prodigal son, but the scorn and jealousy of the older brother created a wall that made their common life tense and unbearable.

The celebration of others demands that we meet the next moment with new perception and an open heart, that we leave behind us the dust of former quarrels and bickerings and unpleasant encounters. Celebrating people requires that we re-open the path that disappointment has closed and that failure has barricaded. The challenge to our celebration of others is to allow sin and brushes with human weakness, our own and others', to transform us. Contact with the earthiness of our condition can help us to rejoice in the talents and goodwill of others. Humiliations can make us pliable and understanding, and the truth, faced together and affirmed, can free us for the greater things, the more dangerous, deeper risks.

Another gospel story that is about forgiveness and compassion and that is also about celebration is the story of when Jesus was invited to a feast by Simon. He chided Simon because Simon had failed to treat him as a guest, to provide him with water, to kiss him and anoint his head. But Mary Magdalene, the public sinner, was not afraid to show her emotions. Jesus was supposed to shun her advances. He should have known that she was a sinner and therefore unacceptable, but Jesus' integrity and his openness to a personal relationship enabled him to reach out to Mary Magdalene, to acknowledge her as another human being. Her very humanity was rejected by Simon and the others, but it was honoured by Jesus. A celebration took place: Jesus was honoured and Mary was forgiven.

All celebrations are not easy, and this exchange between Jesus and Mary Magdalene reminds us of that. Repentance and forgiveness do not mean the removal of natural reactions, humiliations, angers, hurts, suspicions, distrust; rather they introduce a new patience, a new understanding, a new degree of tolerance, a bending of our pride. All these things are costly, but after the price is paid there is celebration – great celebration. Peace creeps in where hostility dwelt, and the human spirit grows in maturity and wisdom. We discover that we have been deliberately holding peace at bay and have not been able to celebrate. It is only when we sincerely love that we can set aside our pride, our desire to control and to be right, offer forgiveness and admit guilt or complicity.

Developing a forgiving attitude

A forgiving attitude cannot develop as long as certain other attitudes persist, as long as we cling to our self-righteousness and feed on every opportunity to elevate ourselves and to sit in judgement on others. How often do we set ourselves up as the determiner of what is acceptable or honourable, placing on others higher expectations and greater demands than we put on ourselves? In conversation we use the words 'we' and 'they' to ensure alienation. But in a loving environment where we celebrate each other, this sort of attitude cannot exist, people cannot live like that.

Our freedom as human beings is grounded in forgiveness. Each of us repeatedly offends and is offended, each of us is oppressor and oppressed, wounder and wounded. So often we are cemented into our roles and we cannot free ourselves. But forgiveness liberates us. The experience of forgiveness and the celebration that comes from it enables us to understand our own wretchedness and to accept our failures. We are released to go in peace to resume our roles as responsible members of the community.

A celebratory community makes abundance

The body of Christ is a rich biblical metaphor of the Christian community. To learn to be one body is not an easy lesson, but it is a very beautiful one. If one part of this body suffers, then all suffer, if one part rejoices then all rejoice, if one part celebrates, all celebrate. Our lives are closely bound up with other people's lives. This does not mean that we lose our individuality, but that we share a common life, a common ministry, a common calling. Our individuality is enhanced and celebrated as part of the group.

In a community or a celebratory environment, that which appears to be scarce becomes abundant. The gospel gives expression to this in the story about the loaves and fishes. A group gathers around Jesus eager to hear him speak. As he progresses he is aware that people are hungry and that no provision has been made for such a large a group, so Jesus asks his friends to gather up what they can find and of course there are only some fish and some loaves here and there. But these scarce resources are collected and Jesus has them distributed to the crowd, and amazingly there is enough food for everyone. Jesus turns fragmented resources and privately held sustenance into bountiful nourishment. By sharing the meagre amount of food, the people seem to multiply it; by breaking the bread they make more; and there is a transformation where something small and fragmented becomes abundant and whole, and there is the celebration of a shared meal.

In our world today there is scarcity in the midst of plenty. The scarcity is real and the plenty is real, but we can also invent scarcity by keeping our gifts to ourselves and not spreading them around, not sharing them. Jesus shared himself constantly. Take for example the story of the woman who was struggling to get near him in a crowded street. As soon as she reached out to him and touched his garments Jesus stopped and asked 'Who touched me?' People looked at him in surprise because many people had bumped against him as they passed through the crowded street but Jesus recognised a special touch. He said 'Somebody has touched me because power has gone out of me' (Lk 8:46). Jesus did not stop and decide whether or not he would heal this woman. The woman touched him and power flowed out from Jesus to heal her illness. This story tells us, I think, that our gifts are not our own individual possessions but are given as an energy that is a gift for others. A community or loving environment that develops a habit of celebrating and loving and forgiving also tends to develop an overwhelming reservoir of celebration and forgiveness and love and reconciliation, something that automatically blows over and out to others in the community so that there is an outpouring of the gift to the world, a world of pain and suffering.

Celebration is of the heart and of the spirit

The celebration of a community is a mutual embrace. We embrace the strong and the weak, within the community and within each other. We embrace soul and spirit, body and mind. Celebration is something only the heart can do. When we live from the heart, we are free to let go without fear. When we live from the heart, we celebrate the bond of mutual giving and taking with thanksgiving. The heart fully affirms that all belongs to all. So when we live from the heart we forgive from the heart, from the centre, where the offender and the offended are one, where healing has a truth and forgiving is a perfection of celebration. The heart is the place of letting go, the place of healing and thanksgiving, the place of celebration.

We celebrate whatever there is and for no other reason but simply because it *is*. Celebration is our *raison d'être*. That is what we are made for as human beings. This singular command is engraved in our hearts, and whether we understand this or not matters little, whether we agree or disagree makes no difference. In our heart of hearts we know this.

No matter how hard you strike a bell, it will ring: what else is it made for? Even under hammer blows, the faith of the heart rings true. The human heart is made for universal praise, thanksgiving and celebration. As long as we pick and choose, making praise and thanksgiving depend on a whim, we are not yet responding from the heart. But if we respond from the heart, we find the core of our being is in tune with reality, and reality is praiseworthy. The heart sees with a true vision. It sees the ultimate meaning of all – thanksgiving, blessing, celebration – and with clear intentions the heart responds with the ultimate purpose of its life – thanksgiving, blessing, celebration.

Guidelines

1: Prayer

Place yourself in God's presence

2: Breath prayer

| Breathe in: | I want you to be happy |
| Breath out: | Always happy |

3. Reading:

Read a passage from Chapter 3.

4: Scripture

| Phil 4: 4-9 | 'I want you to be happy ...' |
| Jn 13: 11-15 | The Last Supper |

Lk 15: 11-32   'This son of mine was lost and is found...'

Let these words, phrases, scripture passages, stay with you.
Let them draw you into them.
Allow an image to emerge.
Listen to the image.
Talk to the image.

5: Images of celebration

Questions which you may find helpful to evolve images:

- What image of celebration most relates to your experience of celebration?
- Do you have other images of celebration that speak to you?
- How do you celebrate people?
- Can you image it?
- Have you discovered a 'Jenny' in your life?
- If so, how has it affected you?
- Can you image it?
- What helps you to celebrate?
- Is there an image from art, in any of its forms, that brings you a sense of celebration?
- Is there an image from nature that evokes in you the desire to celebrate?
- Is there an image of celebration that brings life to you?
- What beautiful things in life evoke celebration in you?
- Can you image them?

Allow the image to surface.
Allow it to come to your awareness.
Stay with it.
Listen to it. Talk to it.

6: *The journal*

The following questions may help with your writing:

- If someone were to say to you 'What do you mean by celebration?' what would you say?
- What people do you celebrate?
- What people celebrate you?
- What celebrations uplift you?
- How is your sense of celebration restored?
- Remember a time in your life when a celebration experience changed you.
- Was it the celebration of a person? of a group? of work well done? Was it a faith celebration? How did it change you?

7: *Thanks*

Give God thanks for the gift of celebration. Ask for an increase in the spirit of celebration.

Chapter 5

Compassion

Compassion is about living with an open heart. It's about welcoming people, giving them a place in our hearts. It isn't about offering a limited service to one person and then moving on to the next person. It is about opening our hearts and carrying people in our hearts, even at the times when we cannot give them the help they need. Above all else, Christian compassion calls us to honour God with our hearts as we journey through life together.

Acceptance

Living with an open heart implies acceptance. Acceptance is a sign of human and Christian maturity. It is opening our hearts to the other in a way that allows them to grow in freedom and to their full potential. In our services as Christian people, we must accept people as they are, not as we would like them to be. People who are in need are afraid of revealing themselves, of opening up. They need people who will listen to them, with all their wounds and needs. They need to sense that they are not being judged. They need people who will help them to rediscover their self-esteem, self-respect, pride, dignity, and sense of empowerment. But they will not rediscover their own value simply by having the door opened to them; they must also be accepted for what they are. True acceptance and welcome are found not only in the great unusual moments when we experience a very lively sense of renewal; they are equally present in the small gestures of tenderness, forgiveness, humility that are part of everyday life.

Bridging the gap between what we do and who we are

Many of us talk a lot about love and truth and justice but there is still a big gap between what we say and what we do and are. The people who come to us for help because they have been rejected over and over again can see very clearly if there is a gap between what we say and what we do, between our ideals and our reality. It is important that we constantly struggle to bridge that gap between what we say and how we live. If we don't, we will reject people yet again. We will devalue them again, for no other reason than that they have shown up our hypocrisy.

There are times when we are unable to welcome people because of fear, weariness, insecurity, tiredness or just because we have had enough. In situations where we are unable to welcome because we cannot make space for the other it is better that we acknowledge and accept where we are and deal with it and not go on pretending that we are loving and welcoming.

Acknowledging our own weakness

Acknowledging our own weakness, then, is an essential quality for those of us providing a service. We are often so busy protecting ourselves that we are not present or open to people who are wrestling with their sense of weakness, fear and unworthiness. To accept and welcome another means acknowledging our own limitations and weaknesses and our fears and going beyond them to a deeper compassion and understanding. Acknowledging our weakness can soften our defensiveness and can help us to put our trust in God, so that with St Paul we will be able to say that 'my strength is made perfect through weakness'. The more we can acknowledge our vulnerability, the more we can acknowledge our need for God.

It is in pushing us to acknowledge our own weakness that those whom we are helping reveal to us our own vulnerability, our blind spots, those parts of us that are not yet converted, transformed. As the poor reveal to us those parts that are unconverted, we can ask God to heal our woundedness, our brokenness, to give us his unconditional, unlimited, total love that we may be able to love with that love unconditionally and totally.

Love and professionalism

When we welcome people who are deeply wounded, we have to be fully aware of the seriousness of what we are doing. We have to be professional as well as personal and compassionate in our work. The messages of people who are in distress or anguish, who have experienced violence, abuse or depression are very often sent to us through difficult, disturbed and disturbing behaviour. While love is essential in a Christian service, we need more than love if we are to be able to receive these messages. We must try to understand what people are saying to us through their great confusion.

In *Love is not Enough* Bruno Bettelheim stresses the importance of being skilled in what we do as well as being loving. That does not mean that we all have to be therapists, or go through analysis. It does mean, however, that we have to be sensitive to the deep needs of other people, and we have to be aware of the times when we need to call in different kinds of professional help. The Christian helping service that welcomes people in distress must draw on modern sciences and expertise, and it must also develop its own professionalism and therapy based on relationships that are authentic, loving and faithful.

The Christian helping services must be discerning. It must, through prayer and reflection, discover what God is asking or drawing us to, distinguish between the important and the urgent, discern what is essential in a very confused story, be able to suggest steps to be taken on the road to healing. We have to be professional enough to know when and what expertise is needed, and to know whether it is expertise we can offer, or whether we must look elsewhere for it.

Living a life that is dependent on God

If we are to offer compassion through a caring service, we must find a rhythm to our own lives. We must find space and time for ourselves, for our God, for our friends, as well as for the people we live and work with. We have to struggle to live an integrated, seamless life. Having a deep spiritual experience early in the morning and then business as usual for the rest of the day isn't an integrated life. We have to find how to put love and prayerfulness into all our activities, all the reading and writing, all the caring and counselling, all the cleaning and washing up, all the chores we carry out in our daily life. We must understand that it is God's work that we are doing, and so we strive each day to find God in all things, believing that God can work miracles through us. We must do everything as if everything depended on ourselves and pray as if everything depended on God.

'To have seen me is to have seen the Father,' Jesus said, 'and if you believe in me, you will perform the same works as I do myself... You will perform even greater works, because I am going to the Father... Whatever you ask for in my name, I will do so the Father may be glorified in the Son' (Jn 14:7-14). Jesus never mentions the word 'success', but talks about fruitfulness over and over again. As a Christian people, 'If we abide in God, God will abide in us, and we will bear much fruit' (Jn 15). In a very highly competitive society, we can fix our eyes on goals we want to reach and push aside everything that is in the way. We can even do that as we develop services to assist the poor. But as Christians we must try to ensure that the services we offer are fruitful for the people we serve and fruitful for ourselves and the people who serve with us, so that together we can grow into a full life.

Having a clear perspective

Sometimes we can be too busy with God's work and lose sight of what is important for the sake of the urgent and the immediate. When a monk at the Abbey of Clairvaux was elected Pope Eugene III, his former abbot, St Bernard, wrote to him a lengthy letter of love and concern:

> I worry constantly about you; I'm afraid that you will be so trapped in your numerous occupations that you see no way out, and therefore harden yourself defiantly; that you suppress little by little the sense of an appropriate and wholesome grief. It is far wiser for you to withdraw from time to time from your affairs, than let your affairs draw you and drive you, step by step, to where you certainly do not want to go. You ask where? To the point where the heart is hardened. Do not ask any further what this means – if you are not alarmed now, your heart is already there. Those with hardened hearts never attain salvation, unless God took pity on them and took away their hearts of stone and gave them hearts of flesh. To encompass aptly all the evils of this horrible disease in a single phrase: a hardened heart

neither fears God nor respects people. Look: this is where these accursed activities will drag you if you carry on like this and completely lose yourself in them, without reserving some time and energy for yourself. You waste your time, and if I may allow myself to be for you another Jethro, you will wear yourself out this way, in this senseless toil which only afflicts your mind, eats out your heart and squanders God's grace. What after all are the fruits of all this? Are they not mere cobwebs?

(Peter Van Breemen SJ,
from *Let all God's Glory Through*)

These are very strong words, but they are words we can all take to heart ourselves as we strive to do good and to work hard. Are we going to allow our hearts to be softened? Are we going to allow our hearts of stone to turn into hearts of flesh, as Ezekiel said?

Experiencing our own emptiness and powerlessness

Very often those of us who provide services feel we have little to give. We can remind ourselves of Elijah's story, when he met a poor widow gathering sticks. He wanted water, so the widow went to fetch it for him. Then he wanted bread, but she had none. She was gathering sticks to make a fire, to prepare a final meal to eat with her son, out of the handful of flour and few drops of oil she had left, before dying. But the prophet said to her, 'Do not fear. Do as you were planning, but give me some as well, and you will not run out.' The three of them were able to eat for a year, the prophet, the woman and the child. The flour did not vanish, the oil did not go dry.

There are times when we think we have nothing left to give. Little remains in the barrel of our lives when we are worn down. Then for some strange reason, we manage to get more out of the nothing that we have left – a new grace is born. This is the power and the grace of God working through us. It can only happen if we really put our trust in God, and allow God to take over.

We experience that ourselves with people we are helping. We meet somebody who seems outwardly to have little to give – no education, no programme, no sermon, no sound advice, no solution to our problems. But what they have to give us is more important, and it is not from their surplus, but from their substance, all they have to live on. We find that they have offered us their very being, their presence, their hearts; what they bestow on us finally is no merely human gift, but the life of God flourishing in our faith, hope and love. That is the gift of the poor to us.

Being fully present

We can do precisely the same for people when we are truly present to them. Sometimes we are able to do many things for people: we can provide food, shelter, clothes for them, and at the same time we can offer them our hearts. But sometimes we can do very little, and at times there will be nothing we can do. Then we can only be with the person in his or her pain. This can be a more profound healing experience. Hearts that have known pain meet in mutual recognition and trust, and from this the true service of healing and the mutual compassion of hope and love arises.

A living, listening presence

Much of our capacity to help another depends on our state of mind. Being with people, being able to listen, is one of the greatest gifts we can offer another. But to do that, we have to examine the agitation of our own minds. We have to be aware of the chattering that goes on in our minds and find our own quiet space, so that we can really enter into the suffering of another. Judging, thinking, evaluating, leaping in, taking things personally, being bored, being distracted, reacting – these are all part of everybody's lives. Sometimes we are so scattered and distracted that we are not even aware that we are not present, that we are using our minds to try and solve some other problem, that we are only half-listening. There is a pull to fix things, to look for a solution. We feel that our analytical minds must stay on top of everything, and so we jump between listening, judging and fixing. The mind tries to do too many things at once. But in our attempts to help we may increase the distance between ourselves and the person we are with. We can very easily find ourselves in our own thoughts, and not with the other person. The result is that there is less room to meet the other, less room for a new truth to emerge, less room to let things simply be revealed in their own good time.

This kind of agitation is not a surprise to most of us. Many of us have come to expect and accept it, yet it need not be that way. Because of our mind's capacity to think, we tend to believe that thinking is its only attribute, but there is more to the mind than reason. Being aware is a deep quality of the mind. Buddhists have a strong tradition of developing what they call awareness or a listening mind, developing a deeper consciousness, becoming more centred and more focused. We can all develop that deeper consciousness and awareness if we are willing to acknowledge the agitation of our minds, to practise meditation, to access our deeper qualities of mind and in that way deepen our powers to heal and to help. There are several methods that can help us to enter into the surprising possibilities within ourselves.

Inner calm, sharp concentration, deep intuitiveness and understanding, and an ability to tune into the other is a very important part of a helping service. In a helping service, when our awareness remains quiet and clear, we have a breadth of perspective. It is broad and deep and yet it is also focused. With all of this, we are not only thinker-participants, but observers of our thinking and participation as well. When we quiet our minds, it is possible to have an overall awareness of the total situation, including ourselves, and it is possible to enter into a deep union with the person we are helping; and to be deeply and finely tuned in to where they are.

Knowing our own pain

Another important element in a helping Christian service is openness to our own pain. We need to care for ourselves with the very same attention and open-heartedness that we would like to offer others. Opening to our pain, exploring the roots of our own suffering increases our opportunity for growth. This process can also be of immeasurable value in our efforts to be of service to others. As our understanding of our own suffering deepens, we become available at a deeper level to those we care for. Very often we run away from our pain, we hide behind our role, not always realising how much it limits us.

The philosopher Gurdjieff said that if we wish to escape from prison, the first thing we must acknowledge is that we are in prison – without acknowledgement no escape is possible. If we don't recognise that we are entrapped within our roles, then we cannot be open to alternatives. It is only when we are able to step outside our role or situation for a moment and recognise the restrictions that we can even be prepared to acknowledge that somehow we ourselves are contributing to our own sense of imprisonment.

Often there are great expectations of us in our roles, and we try to live up to those expectations without taking into account what is really needed at the time. Sometimes we create these expectations ourselves, without being conscious of them, but the beginning of our escape is being alert to our entrapment. If we allow ourselves to become more alert, we can allow ourselves to open to the fullness of our humanity; we can make room for it all, and as we do this, the richness and reciprocity of helping works to dissolve the barriers created by our roles.

Christian compassion as journey

Helping other people is not some special gift. It is not the domain of rare individuals. The caring impulse is a natural part of everyone, and through our caring, we can develop that caring impulse also in the people we are caring for. It doesn't matter what we are doing – a very simple act can be very precious, depending on how it is given and received. An ordinary act of kindness which any of us can perform can reveal a glimpse of our common divinity. But this only happens when that act of kindness is carried out with a deep consciousness of one another; a deep awareness and respect for each other.

Compassion is a journey that deepens our overall awareness of ourselves and other people and the world around us. It is an awakening to our call, our call to live to the full. The value of such a perspective is not so much that it leads to great experiences, but that it brings with it a great inner peace. Nothing is spiritual just by calling it so, but we know it when we experience it. Very often this experience is revealed to us in what is most familiar to us as human beings, in what we can most readily understand and appreciate. It is always touching, comforting and uplifting. We find in it the power and beauty of a single simple act of caring and of being in the caring. We can of course help through what we do, but the deeper and deepest level of help is simply through who we are and who we are in the doing.

Each of us walks two journeys – the inward journey of faith and of understanding ourselves and the outward journey of living, working and helping others. The two journeys constantly affect each other. As we help others, we are helped ourselves. In this recognition we find new freedom and opportunity – external obstacles and old habits, our past experience, can now be dealt with in a broader context. We no longer see ourselves as totally separate, but as part of a whole. As we take this path, it is neither straight nor smooth; at moments we can become profoundly aware of our oneness with all things, our unity, our sense of the impossible becoming possible, then suddenly a situation arises and we are thrown back into pain and struggle and separateness. This in turn can lead us into a deeper awareness of who we are and where we are going.

The way of transformation and unity

It is through raw struggle and difficulty that transformation takes place. Gradually we come to sense profound changes in who we are; our hearts can open and our awareness expand beyond what we once would deem possible. We can even discover this sense of wholeness and unity in our ordinary work. In demanding situations we may suddenly become conscious of the fact that we are in union with all creation. We may come to recognise how our relationships with others have altered; we may be much more aware of where we are now, what we have in common, than what once seemed to set us apart. As Thomas Merton writes in *Conjectures of a Guilty Bystander*:

In Louisville, at the corner of Fourth and Walnut, in the centre of the shopping district, I was suddenly overwhelmed with the realization that I loved all those people, that they were mine and I theirs, that we could not be alien to one another even though we were total strangers. It was like waking from a dream of separateness, of spurious self-isolation in a special world, the world of renunciation and supposed holiness. The whole illusion of a separate holy existence of a dream. Not that I question the reality of my vocation, or of my monastic life: but the conception of 'separation from the world' that we have in the monastery too easily presents itself as a complete illusion: the illusion that by making vows we become a different species of being, pseudoangels, 'spiritual men', men of interior life, what have you.

Certainly these traditional values are very real, but their reality is not of an order outside everyday existence in a contingent world, nor does it entitle one to despise the secular: though 'out of the world' we are in the same world as everybody else, the world of a bomb, the world of race hatred, the world of technology, the world of mass media, big business, revolution, and all the rest. We take a different attitude to all things, for we belong to God. Yet so does everybody else belong to God. We just happen to be conscious of it, to make a profession out of this consciousness. But does it entitle us to consider ourselves different, or even better, than others? The whole idea is preposterous.

This sense of liberation from an illusory difference was such a relief and such a joy to me that I almost laughed out loud. And I suppose my happiness could have taken form in the words: 'Thank God, thank God'.

In a truly helping service, all is integrated. We are at one with all that is around us. We are a unique part of a whole unity. Awareness of this leads us to a greater compassion for ourselves and for all beings. It enables us to see the beauty of all creation and all humanity in its unity and diversity, its lightness and darkness, its finiteness and infiniteness, its sharing in God. From this vision we have greater willingness and eagerness to reach out to one another with openness. Each day we are moved forward, outward and our consciousness increases, we see our deepest yearnings reflected in others, and this encourages us to believe in our own beauty and in the beauty of others. Each time we reach out with openness we deepen our presence to ourselves and to others and we experience a profound deepening of our intuitiveness and our understanding. Each time we are able to reach out from inside our heart to someone else's pain, despite our fear and defensiveness, we sense a love in us which becomes increasingly unconditional. As we discover our limitations and strengths, our common unity and our diversity, barriers between us and others dissolve.

Compassion not an end in itself

Compassion is therefore part of our journey to unity, not an end in itself. Compassion is a vehicle through which we reach a deeper understanding of life. Each moment we grow towards a greater understanding of ourselves and others and this in turn steadily transforms us again and again into instruments of helping, of service and of healing. Compassion not only means a larger vision of life for us, but it steadily moves us along and supports us in our efforts to realise our own inner journey to knowing ourselves better. Listening more, judging less, there is less divisiveness in us. We loosen our identification with certain roles, with personal motives and models of self, and our awareness becomes more inclusive. We begin to recognise deeper patterns in each person and event as they unfold. This is the essence of our spiritual journey of compassion. Compassion gradually becomes an offering, first to those we are with, but also to God, the source of our being, our loving, our caring. Helping becomes an act of reverence, worship and gratitude. It is a deep grace to serve. Then everything becomes important, the smallest act of filling a bowl of soup and giving it to somebody, of comforting a small child, of listening to a person's story are all means of helping that person, but also means of helping us to grow into a greater unity of life and love, a unity between ourselves and others, a unity within ourselves and a unity between ourselves and God.

Seeing compassion in a spiritual perspective in no way diminishes what we have to offer others through training, experience, individuality, special gifts or skills, or a sense of humour. Quite the reverse – our particular talents and unique skills and qualifications and qualities are likely to come forth more fully when we have a richer and more spacious sense of who we are. Because all is sacred, we are sacred. When we are helping we hold each other's sacredness, because we are all part of the common unity of creation, we are all part of the body of Christ and we all represent Christ to each other.

Guidelines

1: Prayer

Place yourself in God's presence.

2: Breath prayer

| Breathe in: | Compassionate God |
| Breathe out: | Open my heart |

3: Reading

Read a passage from Chapter 5.

4: Scripture

| 1 Jn | 'Think of the love that God has lavished on you.' |

Lk 10: 29-37   The Good Samaritan
Lk 4: 16-21   'Be compassionate ...'
Mk 8: 1-10   'Jesus had compassion on the
                 multitude.'

Let these words, phrases, scripture passages, stay with you.
Let them draw you into them.
Allow an image to emerge.
Listen to the image.
Talk to the image.

5: Images of compassion

Questions which you may find helpful to evolve images:

- What image of compassion most relates to your experience of compassion?
- Do you have other images of compassion that speak to you?
- What image of compassion do you bring to the world?
- Can you image it?
- What images emerge for you when you think of compassion and professionalism?
- What image do you have of the unity between all people?
- What image do you have of us all belonging to God?
- What image do you have of the pain of compassion?
- What keeps you from giving in when your efforts to be compassionate are not responded to? Can you image it?

- Is there an image from music that brings compassion to your heart?
- Is there an image from art, in any of its forms, that brings you a sense of compassion?
- Is there an image from nature that evokes in you compassion?
- What beautiful things in life evoke compassion in you?
- Can you image them?

Allow the image to surface.
Allow it to come into your awareness.
Stay with it.
Listen to it.
Talk to it.

6: The journal

The following questions may help with your writing:
- If someone were to say to you, 'What do you understand by compassion?' what would you say?
- In what way has God been compassionate towards you?
- What makes you compassionate?
- How compassionate are you in relation to the people around you?
- Have they helped you to be more compassionate or have you held them to yourself?
- How compassionate are you when you are busy and overworked?
- What needs to happen in your life to enable you to be more open and receptive and more compassionate?

- Are there people or events in your life that have encouraged and deepened your compassion?
- What is it that keeps you from being compassionate?
- What has happened when you felt people were not compassionate towards you?
- What happens when you feel you are not being compassionate, or have not been compassionate?
- What happens when you feel you have lost your sense of compassion?
- How have you restored that compassion?
- Remember a time in your life when you felt your compassion was being restored.
- Remember a time in your life when people were compassionate towards you and you were unable to accept it.
- Remember a time in your life when people were compassionate towards you and you became more compassionate.

7: Thanks

Give thanks to God for the gift of compassion that you have experienced in your life. Ask God to make you more compassionate.

Chapter 6

Gratitude

Discovering our true identities

We need the grace of poverty of spirit, which is also the grace of gratitude, to discover our true identities, our true selves. Today we hear a lot of talk about 'finding ourselves', discovering ourselves, redesigning ourselves, as if there was something that we could finally possess if we could just peel away enough layers of our life to see it. At times we are tempted to make the self our most precious possession; but if we are to become truly free for the future, we must discover our true identity, which is created by God rather than manufactured by us.

My identity is that I am of God, with God and for God. This identity Thomas Merton has described as 'beyond all social fabrications'. He says:

> At the centre of my being is a point of pure nothingness, which is untouched by sin and by illusion; a point of pure truth, a point or spark which belongs entirely to God, which

is never at our disposal, for which God disposes of our lives, which is inaccessible to the fantasies of our own mind, or the brutalities of our own will. This is the point of nothingness and of absolute poverty; it is the pure glory of God in us (*Conjectures of a Guilty Bystander*).

Learning gratitude from the poor

One way to discover the true self is by working closely with the poor people who have not had much, or who have lost what they had. I have worked with the poor for over thirty years now, and they have taught me many things, but above all, they have taught me to be grateful. They point out all the good things that have been given to us, and how much we take them for granted.

A group of people I know and live among include many who have experienced homelessness, poverty, depression and exclusion. During the past year, I have had the privilege of sharing with them prayers, liturgies and rituals, using symbols and activities to deepen our communal sense of gratitude. What struck me more than anything else was the extraordinary way in which that group was able to name and claim the moments of grace and gratitude in their lives. They were not calculating or doing cost/benefit analyses of their lives; they were simply acknowledging and recognising and being grateful for everything they had. Together, we were setting down small islands of hope, of celebrations, to help us keep sight of God's great love.

During those liturgies and rituals, I began to realise very clearly that grace comes to us when we begin to appreciate the goodness that is already ours. Even if what we possess does not include many material goods, as we experience gratitude, the good expands and so does our sense of gratitude. During those rituals, we were able to acknowledge moments of gratitude for people who walked with us through life, for those who stood beside us when our hopes were small, for those who walked with us when we had nothing but sorrow and death, for those who celebrated our emptiness, for those who broke bread with us and shared with us new life.

Gratitude is an awareness of life

Gratitude is the grounding in the present that connects us with the deepest points of our lives and the furthest points of our future. Henri Nouwen described it like this:

> Gratitude is the awareness that life, in all it manifestations, is a gift for which we want to give thanks. The closer we come to God in prayer, the more we become aware of the abundance of God's gifts to us. We may even discover the presence of these gifts in the midst of our pains and sorrows. The mystery of our spiritual life is that many of the events, people and situations that for a long time seemed to inhibit our way to God become ways of being united more deeply with him. What seems to be a hindrance proves to be a

gift. Thus gratitude becomes a quality of our lives, and allows us to live joyfully and peacefully, even though our struggles continue.

> *A cry for mercy – Prayers from Genesee*
> Henri Nouwen, New York, Image Books,
> Doubleday 1991

Gratitude and greed are mutually exclusive. The way to heal a greedy heart, an envious heart, is to replace it with a grateful heart. When gratitude becomes our way of life, we make peace with our greed and with our envy, not excusing it or ignoring it, but acknowledging it as part of ourselves. Then with the Psalmist we can pray:

> It was you who created my innermost being, and put me together in my mother's womb. For all these mysteries, I thank you for the wonder of myself and for the wonder of your works.

> Ps 129:13-14

One of the purposes of prayer is to remind us of the gracious generosity of God and to awaken in us a sense of appreciation for the goodness that is already ours. Prayer moves us deeply into the mystery of grace, and prayer will open ourselves to the abundance of God. Here our emptiness becomes a gift rather than a disappointment, as God fills us with love. The more needy we are, the more we know our need for God. And in humility we begin to recognise the gifts and graces bestowed on us over our lifetime.

Gratitude helps us to live in interdependence

Sometimes we find it difficult to be grateful for something, because we have difficulty in acknowledging that it is a gift. My mother used to express her thanks by saying, 'I am much obliged.' We hardly ever hear people saying that today, and that is because people don't want to be obliged, don't like acknowledging their dependence on other people. There is of course a healthy side to this desire to be independent, self-sufficient. To grow up means learning to help ourselves, but it is also part of being truly grown up, fully mature, to be able to accept help when we need it and acknowledge that help when we get it. Some people never seem to grow beyond the stage of wanting to do everything themselves.

Self-sufficiency is an illusion, and sooner or later, life will shatter that illusion. None of us would be who we are or where we are if it were not for our parents, or our teachers, or our friends, or somebody in our lives. Even our enemies help to make us who we are and what we are. There are no self-made people. Every one of us needs others. Sooner or later, life brings this truth home to us. It may be a sickness, it may be a breakdown in relationships, it may be a broken marriage, it may be a sudden bereavement, it may be a long, lingering illness, but in some way life catches us by surprise.

Nobody wants to live under obligation or in total dependence, but total *in*dependence is an illusion, because none of us can live completely independently. If we are trying to choose between dependence and independence, we are in trouble. The choice is really between living in alienation and living in interdependence. Total independence is alienation, because we are cut off from others, but mere dependence is a type of alienation too, because total dependence is slavery and the slave is an alien.

Interdependence, on the other hand, joins us with others through the bond of joyful giving and taking. Dependence ties us with ties of slavery; independence ties us with bonds of illusion; but the bonds of interdependence are ties that set us free. One single gift, acknowledged in gratefulness, has the power to dissolve the ties of alienation, and we are free, home, where all depend on all.

Thanks is the greatest gift

The interdependence of gratefulness is truly mutual. The receiver of the gift depends on the giver, but the circle of gratefulness is incomplete until the giver and the gift become the receiver – the receiver of thanks. When we give thanks, we give something greater than the gift we received, whatever it is. The greatest gift we can give is thanksgiving. In giving gifts, we often give what we can spare, but in giving thanks, we give ourselves. The one who says 'Thank you' to another really says 'We belong together.' The giver and the thanksgiver belong to each other. The bond units them and frees them from alienation.

Surprised by joy

Occasionally, when we least expect it, a grace we have long needed comes to us, and like Wordsworth, we are 'surprised by joy'. Even our sufferings and losses become occasions of grace, when we recognise through them the sufferings and losses of others, but also when we realise we are not abandoned, even if we abandon ourselves.

Wherever we may be, we are in some way engaged in universal give and take. If our feelings are too scarred and too jaded to fully vibrate to the great giving and receiving, we might at least find one small area in which we can spontaneously respond with joy.

Life is full of surprises, and surprise is the key to gratitude. No matter how trapped we may be, surprise discloses, and even if our life lacks the surprise of the extraordinary, the ordinary can always be surprising. A fresh look at the ordinary can be the greatest surprise of all. 'Nature is never spent,' Gerard Manley Hopkins says as he praises God's grandeur, and 'There lives the dearest freshness deep-down things.'

The surprise of the unexpected will wear of, but the surprise of that freshness never wears off. In rainbows, it is obvious. Less obvious is the surprise of freshness present in the most ordinary things, but we can learn to see it as plainly as we see rainbows. Sometimes we have to train ourselves at spotting it. Robert Frost calls it 'a mist from the breath of a wind/a tarnish that goes at the touch of a hand'.

There is a sense of wonder in us that we have

strongly when we are children, but many of us have lost it as we grew up. The child is always surprised. If you walk with a child, you notice how everything surprises them, the least thing. It may be that we 'saw this morning morning's minion,' as Gerard Manley Hopkins says, 'dapple-dawn-drawn falcon in his riding,' or it may be that we saw it in the eyes of a woman that was homeless as she entered for the first time into her new home – a great sense of joy, surprise, amazement, gratitude.

Surprise is the source of gratitude

An inch of surprise can lead to miles of gratefulness. To recognise surprise is the beginning and the source of gratitude. In moments of surprise we catch a glimpse of the joy to which gratefulness opens the door.

Surprise in the full sense means gratefulness. Even the predictable turns into a surprise the moment we stop taking it for granted. If we knew how the whole world worked, we could still be surprised that there was a universe at all, but if we don't think about it, we won't be surprised at it. Our eyes are open to the surprise in the world around us the moment we wake up from taking things for granted.

Things or events can trigger our surprise, but they are merely catalysts. We all have to find what triggers surprise for us. e. e. cummings says 'the eyes of my eyes are opened' and we can all train ourselves to become more and more awakened, and to remain awake.

Gratitude is a way of being alive

Gratefulness is the measure of our aliveness. If we are numb, if we take things for granted, then we are dead, because to those who are awake to life's surprises, death lies behind, not ahead. To live life open to surprise, in spite of all that's dying around us, makes us even more alive.

Surprise is a growth process, one that we have to develop. This year, our new little garden at the Lodge in Stanhope Green began to show for the first time little signs of life – a single crocus blossom. We waited for them, but still it was a surprise to see the shoot coming up through the earth that never had a shoot before. It was enough to convince us that springtime had come and that no matter how predictable the spring is, it is a gift of grace.

Gratitude keeps us youthful. By being more and more grateful, we get younger every day. Surprise is the starting point. It opens our inner eye, because the amazing fact is that everything is a gift. Nothing can be taken for granted. If it can't be taken for granted, then we must be grateful. And as we begin to be grateful for small things, that gratitude grows and grows and expands and expands, like expanding ripples on the surface of a pool. What starts it off may be a little stone, a little surprise, a little openness, and as the ripple expands, it becomes more and more alive to what is given, more and more alive to the giver, and more and more alive to giving.

Guidelines

1: Prayer

Place yourself in God's presence

2: Breath prayer

Breathe in: Thank you, Thank you, God
Breathe out: For everything

3: Reading

Read a passage from Chapter 3.

4: Scripture

2 Cor 1:3-4	'Blessed be the God and Father of our Lord Jesus Christ…'
Eph 3:20-21	'Glory to God who shows his power in us…'
2 Cor 2:14-17	'Thanks be to God who always leads us in triumphant following of Christ…'

Let these words, phrases, scripture passages, stay with you.
Let them draw you into them.
Allow an image to emerge.
Listen to the image.
Talk to the image.

5: Images of gratitude

Questions which you may find helpful to evolve images

- What image of gratitude most relates to your experience of gratitude today?
- Do you have other images of gratitude that speak to you?
- What is your image of surprise?
- Have you been surprised by God? Can you image it?
- Have you been surprised by joy?
- If you have, what is your image of it and how has it affected you?
- What happened in order for you to discover that surprise?
- What keeps that surprise alive in you?
- What happens when you stop being grateful? Can you image it?
- What keeps you from being grateful? Can you image it?
- Is there an image from music that brings surprise or gratitude to your heart?
- Is there an image from nature that evokes in you gratitude or surprise?
- What beautiful things in life evoke gratitude in you?

Allow the image to surface.
Allow it to come into your awareness.
Stay with it.
Listen to it.
Talk to it.

6: The journal

The following questions may help with your writing:

- If someone were so say to you 'What do you understand by gratitude' what would you say?
- What do you understand by surprise?
- What are the things or people that evoke gratitude in you?
- What are the people, situations or experiences that surprise you?
- What keeps you from being grateful?
- What keeps you from being surprised?
- What happens when you feel you are losing your sense of gratitude?
- Can you remember a time in your life when that gratitude was restored?
- What happens when you feel you are losing your sense of surprise?
- When you have lost your sense of surprise how have you restored it?
- Can you remember a time in your life when gratitude was restored?
- How did it happen?
- Was it through a person, an experience, or through your faith in God?
- Have you a memory of being filled with gratitude?
- Have you a memory of a person who radiates with a heart full of gratitude?

7: Thanks

Make a list of what you are grateful for today, give God thanks and ask for an increase of gratitude.

Printed in Italy
by AGAM s.r.l. - Madonna dell'Olmo - Cuneo
October 1999